TOP CLASS

Punctuation

Year 5

Now supported with CPD training
For info visit www.johnmurraycpd.co.uk

Hopscotch
A division of MA Education Ltd

John Murray

Published by Hopscotch, a division of MA Education, St Jude's Church, Dulwich Road, London, SE24 0PB
www.hopscotchbooks.com
020 7738 5454

©2015 MA Education Ltd

Written by John Murray

Series designed by Claire White, Fonthill Creative, 01722 717029

Cover illustration by Sara Anderton
www.catandfoxadventures.com

Illustrations by Emma Turner

Associate Publisher: Angela Morano Shaw

ISBN 9781909860193

All rights reserved. This resource is sold subject to the condition that it shall not, by way of trade or otherwise, be lent, hired out or otherwise circulated without the publisher's prior consent in any form of binding or cover other than that in which it is published and without a similar condition, including this condition, being imposed upon the subsequent purchaser.

No part of this publication may be reproduced, stored in a retrieval system, or transmitted, in any form or by any means, electronic, mechanical, photocopying, recording or otherwise, without the prior permission of the publisher, except where photocopying for educational purposes within the school or other educational establishment that has purchased this book is expressly permitted in the text.

Every effort has been made to trace the owners of copyright of material in this book and the publisher apologises for any inadvertent omissions. Any persons claiming copyright for any material should contact the publisher who will be happy to pay the permission fees agreed between them and who will amend the

Contents Page

Introduction _____ 6

Capital Letters _____ 8

Full Stops _____ 12

Question Marks _____ 16

Exclamation Marks _____ 20

Commas I (within lists) _____ 24

Commas II (within clauses) _____ 28

Inverted Commas _____ 32

Apostrophes (for omission) _____ 36

Apostrophes (for possession) _____ 40

Brackets _____ 44

Ellipses _____ 48

Colons _____ 52

Semi-colons _____ 56

Punctuation for Parenthesis _____ 60

Introduction

Top Class is a series that endeavours to combine traditional approaches to the teaching and learning of grammar, punctuation and vocabulary with new techniques and activities that support and encourage good learning.

The three core areas have been separated into three distinct books aimed primarily at Key Stage 2. The three books ought to be used in conjunction with each other in order to provide learners with a wider learning environment and for them to understand that these core elements of Literacy work together and are not to be applied in isolation.

Specific elements of the new Key Stage 3 National Curriculum have also been included in order to introduce Key Stage 2 learners to more complex grammatical constructions and vocabulary as they make their transition from attaining Level 4 to Level 5 in writing.

Each book, one for each Year group in Key Stage 2, aims to promote discussion about specific areas of Literacy and provide experiences and opportunities to use and apply what they have learnt.

The three books are as follows:

- **Top Class – Grammar**
- **Top Class – Punctuation**
- **Top Class – Vocabulary**

Each book contains lessons that develop a 'top-down' approach, allowing learners to see how we use language in context, not simply *when* we use a particular word, punctuation mark or grammatical construct but *how* to use it to its best effect when writing independently.

As such, it actively promotes the core principle that to learn grammar and punctuation well and to extend your personal vocabulary effectively, then you must not only see these particular elements of Literacy within authentic and meaningful context and settings but you must then have the opportunity to apply what you have understood in your own independent writing.

All too often children are taught grammar, punctuation and vocabulary with exercises that aren't rooted within an authentic experience; and, as a result, although they may gain full marks in their exercise books, they often misapply or omit what has been learnt in their own free writing.

The *Top Class* series seeks to address this problem using a three staged approach, each Lesson Plan being structured so that learners are encouraged to investigate and explore the English language; initially with support and guidance from their teacher and fellow peers before being asked to apply what they have learnt as individuals.

Think about...

Before undertaking the Guided activity, learners are asked about what they already know about a particular piece of punctuation or grammatical form and where they might have seen it.

This links directly to the Guided text, again helping learners to view grammar, punctuation and vocabulary in context, housing it so that stronger links can be made with prior learning and personal experiences. This can then be used as a springboard to explore and develop this further in a familiar setting.

For example, when looking at our use of capital letters when writing a proper noun, learners may be asked about why people use an atlas or map before looking at a tourist map of London and considering why place names and famous tourist attractions start with a capital letter.

Guided

This is a shared activity that engages the whole class.

Set within a specific and relevant genre of Literacy, it embeds each particular piece of grammar, punctuation or vocabulary being taught in a focused and meaningful way. Moreover, it invites learners to use this information in order to answer a series of questions that are related to the text itself and then begins to move beyond it.

Each of the three questions asked have been carefully formatted so that valuable practice for the end of *Key Stage 2 English grammar, punctuation and spelling test* can be undertaken throughout each Year group. Marks are also available so that pupils gain practice at providing fuller explanations for those questions where two or three marks are being awarded. Answers are provided on the Lesson Plan.

Independent

This activity can be completed as an individual, with a partner or within a small group.

Each Independent activity within the book is also differentiated at an upper and lower level* and offers teachers a range of practical activities that support learners as they practice what they have learnt in the Guided section.

*Differentiated activities can be found on the CD Rom.

Homework

Included in this section is a homework activity that aims to encourage wider learning outside of the classroom to take place. There are two types of homework activities that are provided, each having been designed to help learners discover and engage with grammar, punctuation and vocabulary in the 'real' world:

A] Specific 'closed' questions may be asked in order that research skills, both modern and traditional, can be employed to find a particular answer.

For example: What is the capital city of Demark? Who was the first man to walk on the moon? When necessary, answers are provided on the Lesson Plan.

B] Wider 'open' tasks are given in order to afford learners the opportunity to explore the world around them and collect examples that are both pertinent and authentic.

For example, learners may be asked to find three examples where a shop's name uses an **apostrophe** in their local high street.

Extension

This final stage of the learning journey is an important one and underscores the importance of using a 'top-down' approach to the teaching and learning of grammar, punctuation and vocabulary.

Each Extension activity within the book is also differentiated at an upper and lower level.*

Its aim is to encourage children to apply what they have learnt in a meaningful and purposeful way in order to embed their learning.

For example, learners may be asked to write a shopping list when planning a party that will naturally include a colon or use strong adjectives to describe a certain event in a story.

More importantly, it is this *writing for purpose* (rather than to score arbitrary marks or achieve irrelevant ticks in an exercise book) that provides a meaningful opportunity for individuals to engage with the English language and create their own work that uses grammar, punctuation and vocabulary in a way that brings their work to life.

In this way, not only will each learner be encouraged to use particular forms of grammar, punctuation or vocabulary correctly but, essentially, they will gain a strong sense of themselves taking an active role as a writer. It gives them a valuable sense of what it is like to be an author, one who uses grammar not only to improve the quality of their work but also to express themselves as best they can using the written word.

The journey from simply understanding how the English language works to being able to apply that knowledge in order to become a capable and confident writer is a journey that will continue into adulthood and one that, in all truthfulness, never really ends.

However, by providing meaningful activities for both the classroom and beyond, the *Top Class* series can help each and every writer to freely use grammar, punctuation and vocabulary to great effect and support them as they endeavour to bring the written word to life in order to inform, influence and entertain their readers.

Differentiated activities can be found on the CD Rom.

Capital Letters

Think about...
What do you know about Henry VIII?
Look at the mnemonic about his wives:
"Divorced, beheaded, died, divorced, beheaded...
survived!"
What might this tell us about King Henry VIII?

Guided

Imagine you are a Tudor and want to interview each of King Henry's six wives.

Which wife would you like to talk to first? Why? With a partner choose one to interview and write four questions you would like to ask. What might the answer to each of your questions be?

Once done, find another pair who would like to interview a different wife and compare your questions. Then answer the questions on page 9.

Independent

Read the biographical extract about Henry VIII before he became King.

On your own, with a partner or in a small group; complete the task sheet provided to you by your teacher on page 10.

Once finished, cut off the homework task to take home with you for further practice.

Extension

Write a short biography about your favourite King or Queen. Complete the task sheet on page 11.

Once completed, compare their reign with that of Henry VIII.

Answers

1 Castles: 1 2 3 [4] 5
Kimbolton Castle; Windsor Castle; Kendal Castle; Sudeley Castle.
Palaces: 1 2 3 4 [5]
Greenwich Palace; Whitehall Palace; Hampton Court Palace; Chelsea Old Palace; Oatlands Palace.

2 Religious Buildings: 1 2 3 [4] 5
Peterborough Cathedral; Westminster Abbey; Chapel of St. Peter; St. George's Chapel.

3 Düsseldorf – Germany
Alcalá de Henares – Spain

Homework

- King George VI died on February 6th, 1952, while Princess Elizabeth and Prince Philip were touring Kenya and she immediately became Queen.

- After months of preparation, Queen Elizabeth II was crowned at Westminster Abbey on June 2nd, 1953, the first coronation to be broadcast on TV.

Remember...
We use a **capital letter** for the names of people and places of interest, including countries, counties, towns and cities. Special buildings such as castles, churches and palaces also use a capital to start their name.

Capital Letters

www.tudortimes.com | The Six Wives of Henry VIII

"Divorced, beheaded, died... divorced, beheaded, survived!"

1. Catherine of Aragon
Born: 16th December, 1485; Alcalá de Henares, Spain
Married Henry: 11th June, 1509; Greenwich Palace, London
Marriage Dissolved: 23rd May, 1533
Died: 7th January, 1536; Kimbolton Castle
Buried: Peterborough Cathedral

2. Anne Boleyn
Born: circa 1500-1502; Blickling Hall, Norfolk
Married Henry: 25th January, 1533
Divorced: 17th May, 1536
Executed: 19th May, 1536; Tower of London
Buried: Chapel of St. Peter, Tower of London

3. Jane Seymour
Born: circa 1507-1509; Wolf Hall, Wiltshire
Married Henry: 30th May, 1536; Whitehall Palace, London
Died: 24th October, 1537; Hampton Court Palace
Buried: St. George's Chapel, Windsor Castle

4. Anne of Cleves
Born: 22nd September, 1515; Düsseldorf, Germany
Married Henry: 6th January, 1540; Greenwich Palace, London
Divorced: 9th July, 1540
Died: 16th July, 1557; Chelsea Old Palace, London
Buried: Westminster Abbey

5. Catherine Howard
Born: circa 1525
Married Henry: 28th July, 1540; Oatlands Palace, London.
Executed: 13th Feb, 1542; Tower of London
Buried: Chapel of St. Peter, Tower of London

6. Catherine Parr
Born: circa 1512; Kendal Castle, Cumbria or Blackfriars, London
Married Henry: 12th July, 1543; Hampton Court Palace
Widowed: 28th January, 1547; Palace of Whitehall, London
Died: 5th September, 1548
Buried: Sudeley Castle, Gloucestershire

Look at this web page and answer the questions below.

1 How many castles and palaces can you find?

Castles: 1 2 3 4 5	Palaces: 1 2 3 4 5
Kimbolton Castle	Greenwich Palace

4 marks

2 How many religious buildings can you find?

Religious Buildings: 1 2 3 4 5
Peterborough Cathedral

3 marks

3 In which country would you find the following two cities?

Düsseldorf: [ ]   Alcalá de Henares: [ ]

2 marks

TOP CLASS - Punctuation - Year 5

Capital Letters

Read this biographical extract about Henry VIII's life before he became king. Use the information to fill in key information on the timeline below.
Don't forget to use a capital letter when you need to.

Fact File:

From Prince to King:

1491:

1501:

1509:

Born June 28th, 1491 in Greenwich Palace, Henry Tudor was the second son of King Henry VII and Elizabeth of York.

Unlike his sickly older brother Arthur, Henry was a healthy, athletic youngster who loved sport and riding horses. He was both artistic and musical too!* Yet it was Arthur, as the eldest son, that was being raised as heir to the throne. Henry, on the other hand, was to enter the church and, as such, received an excellent education. He even learnt to speak several languages: Latin, French, Spanish and Greek.

However, when Henry was ten years old, his pathway into priesthood would change dramatically. His brother Arthur died and Henry (as the sole male heir) was named Crown Prince.

Seven years later, King Henry VII died and Henry immediately sought to marry his brother's former wife, Catherine of Aragon, Princess of Spain.

Soon after their hasty marriage the couple were to be crowned King and Queen of England. On June 23rd (1509) Henry led Catherine from the Tower of London to Westminster Abbey for the coronation to take place. And so began one of the most turbulent reigns Britain has ever seen.

Some believe that the classical tune Green Sleeves was composed by Henry VIII for his future wife Anne Boleyn.

Homework

Find out about Queen Elizabeth II.
- When did she become Queen? Why?
- Where was she when this happened?
- Where did her coronation take place?
- What was so special about this event?

Capital Letters

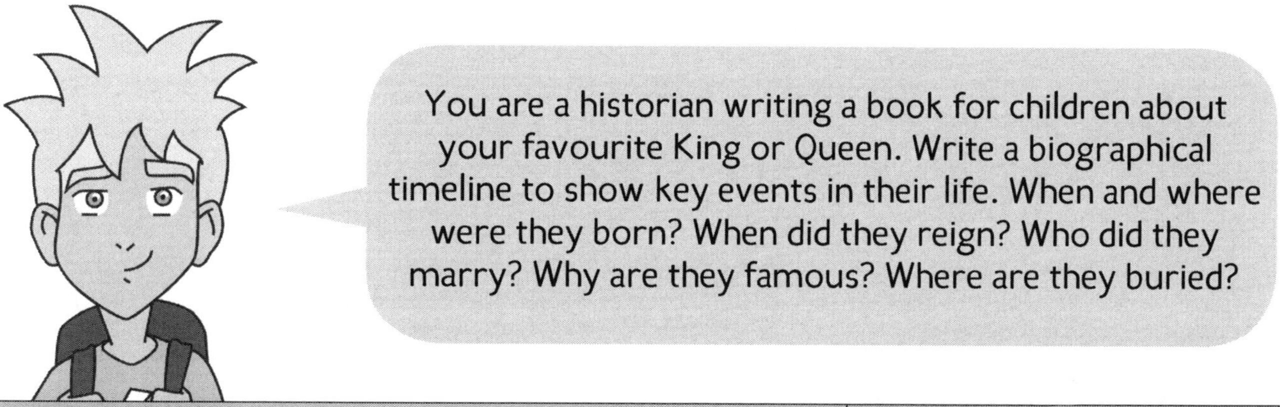

You are a historian writing a book for children about your favourite King or Queen. Write a biographical timeline to show key events in their life. When and where were they born? When did they reign? Who did they marry? Why are they famous? Where are they buried?

Name: **Date:**

Born:

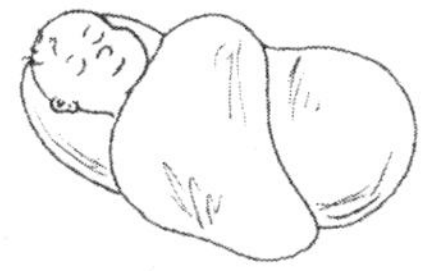

Died:

Full Stops

Think about...
Have you heard of a book called 'The Jungle Book'?
Yes: What do you already know about it?
No: What do you think it might be about?
Would you rather read the book or watch the film? Why?

Guided

Read an extract from the beginning of 'The Jungle Book' by Rudyard Kipling.

Where is this scene set? Which characters are present? What characteristics do they have? What will happen if another member of the Pack does not accept the man's cub? What do you think will happen next?

Discuss your ideas with your teacher, providing evidence from the text itself. Then answer the questions on page 13.

Independent

Read a review of 'The Jungle Book' by a reluctant reader who listened to the story as an audio book instead.

On your own, with a partner or in a small group; complete the task sheet provided to you by your teacher on page 14.

Once finished, cut off the homework task to take home with you for further practice.

Extension

Read a short story and review it for a school magazine. Complete the task sheet on page 15.

Publish and share your review with your classmates.

Answers

1 Three sentences

2 Four sentences

3 There was no answer. Mother Wolf got ready for what she knew would be her last fight, if things came to fighting.

Homework

- First published as a series of short stories in magazines (1893-1894) they were gathered together in *The Jungle Book* in 1894.
- India
- Rudyard Kipling (December 30th 1865 – January 18th 1936)
- Yes: The Walt Disney cartoon adaptation (1967).

Remember...
We use a **full stop** to mark the end of a sentence.

Full Stops

The Jungle Book
By Rudyard Kipling

Now, the Law of the Jungle lays down that if there is any dispute as to the right of a cub to be accepted by the Pack, he must be spoken for by at least two members of the Pack who are not his father and mother.

"Who speaks for this cub?" said Akela. "Among the Free People who speaks?" There was no answer and Mother Wolf got ready for what she knew would be her last fight, if things came to fighting.

Then the only other creature who is allowed at the Pack Council - Baloo, the sleepy brown bear who teaches the wolf cubs the Law of the Jungle: old Baloo, who can come and go where he pleases because he eats only nuts and roots and honey - rose upon his hind quarters and grunted.

"The man's cub - the man's cub?" he said. "I speak for the man's cub. There is no harm in a man's cub. I have no gift of words, but I speak the truth. Let him run with the Pack, and be entered with the others. I myself will teach him."

"We need yet another," said Akela. "Baloo has spoken, and he is our teacher for the young cubs. Who speaks besides Baloo?"

A black shadow dropped down into the circle. It was Bagheera the Black Panther, inky black all over, but with the panther markings showing up in certain lights like the pattern of watered silk. Everybody knew Bagheera, and nobody cared to cross his path; for he was as cunning as Tabaqui, as bold as the wild buffalo, and as reckless as the wounded elephant. But he had a voice as soft as wild honey dripping from a tree, and a skin softer than down.

Look at this children's classic and answer the questions below.

1 How many sentences are there in paragraph two?

One sentence	Two sentences	Three sentences	Four sentences

1 mark

2 How many sentences are there in the final paragraph?

One sentence	Two sentences	Three sentences	Four sentences

1 mark

3 Rewrite this sentence so that it is two sentences.

There was no answer and Mother Wolf got ready for what she knew would be her last fight, if things came to fighting.

_____

_____

2 marks

TOP CLASS - Punctuation - Year 5

Full Stops

Jack has listened to Rudyard Kipling's classic as an audio book.
Here is what he thought about his experience and the book itself. However, he has forgotten to include full stops. Can you help him? There are eight full stops for you to find.

A Review:

Reviewer: Jack (aged 9)
Book Reviewed: The Jungle Book   **Author:** Rudyard Kipling

I'll be honest; I'm not a huge fan of books
   I tend to pick up short stories and comics to read rather than try and wade through a three hundred and fifty page door stopper It's too daunting to think that I'm going to be submerged inside a story for weeks before finding out how it finally ends So when someone suggested I listen to the audio version of this classic instead, I jumped at the chance!
   As this was my first experience of listening to an audio book, I wasn't sure what to expect but the characters and setting came alive The actors and sound effects helped me paint pictures in my mind and imagine the story in much the same way as if I was reading the book It was as though I was in the jungle itself!
   Although, at times, the language was quite difficult (it took me some time to work out 'thou' and 'ye' meant 'you') the story itself was easy to follow and I really enjoyed travelling with Mowgli on his adventures. In fact the ending really saddened me but I won't spoil it for you if you haven't read the book yet
   My favourite character was Bagheera (the Black Panther) as you never quite knew if you could trust him and it was interesting to think that lots of other characters in the story felt the same way as I did
   Overall, this was an awesome experience for me and I would highly recommend not only picking up The Jungle Book but also trying out audio books too! Who knows, next time I may read the book I'm listening to at the same time and see what that's like

---

Homework

Find out about 'The Jungle Book'.
- When was this first published?
- In which country is it set?
- When did Rudyard Kipling a) live b) die?
- Has the book been adapted into a cartoon?

Full Stops

You want to review a book for your school magazine. Think carefully about your audience and why you are writing for them. Which book have you chosen? Why did you choose this book and not another? What aspects of the book would you praise?

Name: _____ **Date:** _____

My Reading Review

Today we read: _____

Author:
First Published:
Published by:
Illustrated by:

Plot Summary: _____
_____
_____

Genre of Text:	Audience:	Message or Theme:
	Young children Older children Teens	

Word Difficulty

1	2	3	4	5	6	7	8	9	10

Too easy — Too hard

1	2	3	4	5	6	7	8	9	10

Too simplistic — Absolutely fantastic

How did this text make you feel?
_____

Why do you think it had this effect on you?
_____
_____
_____

Would you recommend this book to others?   ✓ Yes ☐   ✗ No ☐

Why? ....
....

I'd give this book _____ stars: ☆ ☆ ☆ ☆ ☆

TOP CLASS - Punctuation - Year 5

Question Marks

Think about...
What is a riddle? Do you know any riddles?
Why do people tell riddles?
Do certain riddles keep to a particular format?
What do you notice about the riddles we are about to look at?

Guided

Imagine you have been given three riddles to solve. The answer to each is a letter of the alphabet.

With your teacher, try and work out what the answer to each riddle might be. Why is each riddle clever? Can you write an Alphabet Soup riddle of your own? Your answer will be a letter of the alphabet! Use this format to help you:
You will find me in………but never in …………….. What am I?

Once done, answer the questions on page 17.

Answers: 1 = The letter m. 2 = The letter x (note the word play on 'reflect'). 3 = The letter s.

Independent

You are reading an ancient Greek myth and come across the riddle of the Sphinx.

On your own, with a partner or in a small group; complete the task sheet provided to you by your teacher on page 18.

Once finished, cut off the homework task to take home with you for further practice.

Extension

Look up some riddles or write some riddles of your own. Complete the task sheet on page 19.

Once completed, choose your favourite riddle and act it out.

Answers

1 **What** am I?

2 **Can you** reflect upon which letter should appear next in this sequence? (Allow for variations on this answer. For example, a more formal use of '**Are you able to**' is also acceptable)

3 **Who** said that?
What have you done?
Why are you leaving so early?
Whose are those shoes?
Where did I put my keys?

Homework

- Batman
- Dr Edward Nigma (E.Nigma)
- Bill Finger and Dick Sprang
- First appeared: October 1948 in Detective Comics #140

Remember...
We use a **question mark** at the end of a sentence to show that a question has been asked and to invite the reader to think about what the possible answer might be.

16 TOP CLASS - Punctuation - Year 5

Question Marks

A puzzle...a quandary...a riddle you see,
But can you work out what the answer should be?

I appear once in a minute, twice in a moment but never in a thousand years?

Reflect on which letter should appear next in this sequence.

B C D E H
I K O _

You will find me in the sun and the stars but not in the moon, in summer and spring but not autumn or winter.
Who am I?

Look at these riddles and answer the questions below.

1 Which alternative question marker could be used in the third riddle? Tick one box.

when ☐   why ☐   what ☐   where ☐   how ☐   whose ☐

1 mark

2 Change the statement in the second riddle into a question.

_____

1 mark

3 Match the question marker to complete the question.

Who
What
Why
Whose
Where

are those shoes?
are you leaving so early?
said that?
did I put my keys?
have you done?

4 marks

TOP CLASS - Punctuation - Year 5

Question Marks

Here is an extract from a Greek myth that includes, perhaps, the most famous riddle ever written. Luckily, the hero Oedipus solves the riddle for us. Read this account and draw the solution to each part of the riddle. Then explain it in your own words.

The Riddle of the Sphinx:

Oedipus stood perfectly still and stared intently into the eyes of the Sphinx.

'So you wish to proceed do you? Then answer me this…but remember, fail to do so and you will succeed only in becoming my dinner!'

What creature has but one voice, has four legs in the morning, two legs at noon and three in the evening?

Oedipus stepped forward.

'The answer is man. For when he is born, at the dawn of his life, he walks on all fours crawling as babies do. As an adult, in the prime of life, he walks upright with confidence as I do now. But as the sun begins to set on his life, as an old man he supports himself with a stick, walking with frailty and with doubt as old men do.'

Dawn:	Noon:	Dusk:

Homework

Find out about the cartoon character The Riddler.
- Which superhero does he fight?
- What is his real name?
- Who created him?
- When did he first appear?

TOP CLASS - Punctuation - Year 5

Question Marks

You are a Gate Keeper, the guardian of a magical doorway into another world. However, only those who answer your riddle correctly may gain safe passage through. Where does this portal lead? What will your riddle be? What will happen to those who answer incorrectly? Suddenly somebody comes before you!

Name: **Date:**

HALT!

WHO IS IT THAT STANDS BEFORE ME AND WISHES TO PASS?

Exclamation Marks

Think about...
You see a group of monsters on TV.
Discuss the following:
Genre   Setting   Audience   Purpose   Theme
You look at the clock. It's only 4pm!
Do you want to change your answers? Why?

Guided

Imagine you are watching a comedy sketch set on Halloween.

Which characters might you expect to see in such a sketch? Where might the sketch be set? What do you think the main idea of the sketch might be about? Why? What props might also be included in such a sketch? Make a list of all your ideas with your teacher.

Once done, answer the questions on page 21.

Independent

You are a monster visiting friends on Halloween, talking about how ugly human babies are!

On your own, with a partner or in a small group; complete the task sheet provided to you by your teacher on page 22.

Once finished, cut off the homework task to take home with you for further practice.

Extension

You are a script writer. You want to write a comedy sketch set on Halloween.

Complete the task sheet on page 23.

Once completed, in small groups act it out!

Answers

1 1   2   3   4   [5]

2 To show disgust
To show disbelief

3 Nice (it is the word with the least emotional strength and impact)

Homework

- No specific answers are required for this task, though teachers should check that the ideas provided include appropriate exclamation marks to indicate the strong emotions of disgust, shock and disbelief in order to reflect how the baby would feel.

Remember...
We use an **exclamation mark** to show an intense sense of emotion; especially when following a command or when we are angry, shocked or in disbelief. When used at the end of a sentence or after a single word, it implies the user has strong feelings on the subject.

Exclamation Marks

The Little  Monster

'Cauldron's on,' Winnie cackled. 'Who fancies a cuppa?'

The back door opened. Nobody walked in, pulled up a chair and sat down.

'Is the invisible man not coming tonight?' asked Winston.

'He's just sat down next to you. Can't you see... Oh, never mind,' replied Vlad.

Winnie began pouring the tea and looked directly at Harry (the Headless Horseman). 'And mind the carpet; you know what happened last time!'

'Well, you'll never guess who I saw today,' said the voice from nowhere. 'Only the little monster from next door, the one they call "*baby*".'

'Ugh! The one with beautiful blue eyes and the cutest smile you've ever seen? How awful! And most of them are born without teeth!' shuddered Vlad.

'Now I'm not opposed to slime,' Bob (the Blob) continued, 'but that child dribbles everywhere!'

'He plays football?' snarled Winston.

Bob rolled his third eye.

'And I hear they sleep *on* the bed and not *under* it,' said Harry mid-sip.

They all agreed that being human was a dreadful condition to be in.

Winnie got up and plonked the biscuit tin in the centre of the table.

'Custard scream, anyone?'

Look at this comedy sketch and answer the questions below.

1 How many exclamation marks are in this sketch?

1   2   3   4   5

1 mark

2 Why have the exclamation marks been used? Tick two boxes.

To show disgust ☐   To show excitement ☐   To show anger ☐

To show a loud noise ☐   To show disbelief ☐

2 marks

3 Which word is least likely to use an exclamation mark? Tick one box.

Amazing ☐   Terrible ☐   Great ☐   Nice ☐   Fantastic ☐

1 mark

Exclamation Marks

Imagine you are a monster visiting friends chatting about how ugly human babies are! What would you and your friends say? How beautiful do they look? How sweet do they smell? Don't forget to use an exclamation mark to show how horrible you think they are!

Horrid Humans!

 **Winnie the witch:**

 **Glenda the ghost:**

 **Henry the hobgoblin:**

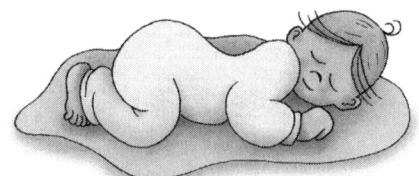

 **Vlad the vampire:**

 **Maggie the mummy:**

 **Zack the zombie:**

Homework

You are the baby and overhear what they say!
- How do you respond?
- What do you do next?
- What do you say?
- How do you feel?

Exclamation Marks

You are a script writer and want to write a comedy sketch for Halloween. A family of humans have just moved next door. The monsters think this is terrible! What do they say about each of the humans? What don't they like about them?

Name:	Date:

Setting:

Winnie the witch:

Glenda the ghost:

Vlad the vampire:

Zack the zombie:

Maggie the mummy:

Henry the hobgoblin:

Commas (within lists)

Think about...
You are about to read the opening of 'The Net'.
What type of story might this be?
Where might it be set? What might it be about?
Who might the main characters be?

Guided

Imagine you are an editor looking at the opening paragraphs of a new thriller called 'The Net'.

Having now read this do you need to change your previous answers? If so, why have you made these changes? Discuss your thoughts with your teacher and your classmates. Are you disappointed or excited about the change in direction this story has taken. Why? What do you think might happen next?

Once done, answer the questions on page 25.

Independent

You are a publisher, looking at notes you have written about books you have been sent to review.

On your own, with a partner or in a small group; complete the task sheet provided to you by your teacher on page 26.

Once finished, cut off the homework task to take home with you for further practice.

Extension

You are the author of 'The Net'. Complete the task sheet on page 27.

Once completed, publish your opening chapter on the computer.

Answers

1   1   2   [3]   4   5

2   Allow for individual response

3   The clouds darkened, the wind howled and I felt the storm wrapping itself around me like a thick cloak of doom.

Homework

- No specific answers are required for this task, though teachers should check that the lists provided by each learner include the necessary commas and an appropriate closing connective.

Remember...
We use a **comma** when we are writing a list to show a break between each item or thought within that list. However, the final two items use a connective such as 'and' between them to note the list is coming to an end.

Commas (within lists)

She had always felt safe swimming with her friends and family; swimming in one direction and with a protective sense of community surrounding her.

But now the waters seemed darker, the currents stronger and a gloom as black as squid ink began to wash over her.

Suddenly, a shadow appeared overhead and she knew she had to leave.

Deeper and deeper she swam, pushing her way forward through a tide of panic and confusion, pressing forward in the hope that it wasn't already too late.

As she neared the edge of the shoal she looked up and saw the net falling.

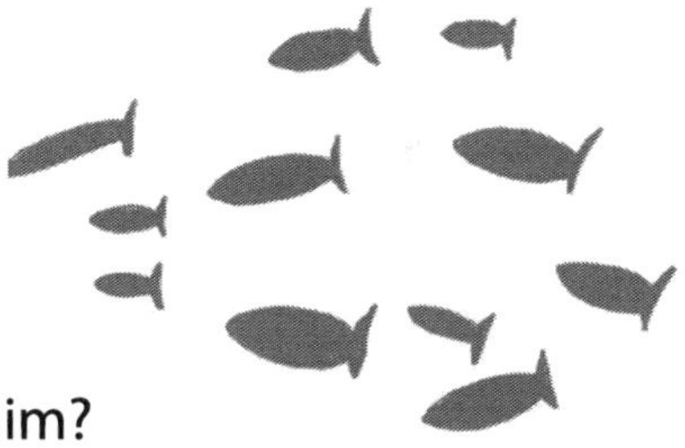

Just then she heard a voice call out to her, 'hey sis, wait for me'.

She glanced into the watery deep before her. Freedom...life!

But how could she forgive herself if she didn't at least try to save him?

'Hurry, we haven't got a second to lose!'

Look at this thriller and answer the questions below.

1 How many things are listed in paragraph two?

1   2   3   4   5

1 mark

2 List five creatures you would find in the ocean using commas.

_____

_____

2 marks

3 Add commas to punctuate the sentence below.

The clouds darkened the wind howled I felt the storm wrapping itself around me like a thick cloak of doom.

2 marks

TOP CLASS - Punctuation - Year 5

Commas (within lists)

You are a publisher writing up notes you have made about different books you have reviewed. Put each set of notes into a single sentence. Don't forget to use a comma between each thought and a connective between the last two.

Notes:

- Heart-warming
- Inspirational
- Empathy with main characters

_____
_____

- Hilarious
- Universal appeal
- Perfect stocking filler for Xmas

_____
_____

- Gripping plot
- Fast paced
- Action packed

_____
_____

- Predictable storyline
- Old fashioned
- Older audience

_____
_____

- Dull
- Seen it all before
- Characters lack depth

_____
_____

_____
_____

Homework

Write a list under the following subjects:
- Three items you might find in a pencil case
- Four presents you might receive on your birthday
- Five creatures you can spot in the North Pole
- Six places you have visited on holiday

Commas (within lists)

You are the writer of 'The Net'! Your editor wants you to write the closing paragraph to your opening chapter. How do you want your story to end?
Do the main characters both escape? How do they feel?
Will you end with a cliff hanger?

Name: **Date:**

THE NET

She glanced into the watery deep before her. Freedom...life!
But how could she forgive herself if she didn't at least try to save him?
'Hurry, we haven't got a second to lose!'

Commas (within clauses)

Think about...
Look at this sentence:
The dog, a Labrador, bit the postman.
Colour the main clause yellow and the secondary clause brown. How do we use commas to show where the embedded clause is?

Guided

You are looking up information on flags as part of a Geography topic.

Why do countries fly flags? Where might you see them? Why are they important? How do they make you feel when you see your own flag? Why? Are there any other flags that you know?

Once done, share your ideas with your teacher. Then answer the questions on page 29.

Independent

Write about what different world flags mean.

On your own, with a partner or in a small group; complete the task sheet provided to you by your teacher on page 30.

Once finished, cut off the homework task to take home with you for further practice.

Extension

Write about your favourite flag. Complete the task sheet on page 31.

Once completed, submit it into a class competition and vote for your favourite design.

Answers

1 Canada's flag also contains a maple leaf, from its national tree, to show that it cares for its nature and the environment.

2 India's flag also contains a special wheel, the Ashok Chakra, which symbolises progress.

3 Sir Edmund Hillary flew the Union Jack when he conquered Mount Everest.

Homework

- No specific answers are required for this task, though teachers should check that each learner has correctly identified the four principle parts of the UK (England, Northern Ireland, Scotland and Wales) and have drawn each flag. Each learner should also have included at least one embedded clause when describing either each individual flag or how they come together to form the Union Jack.

Remember...
When we want to add extra information inside a sentence we can use a comma on either side of that information to show the reader where it is. This extra part of the sentence is often called an **embedded clause**.

TOP CLASS - Punctuation - Year 5

Commas (within clauses)

Flying the Flag

Here are two flags with special symbols on them:

A

B

Adopted on February 15th 1965, Canada's flag has three vertical stripes on it. The two outer stripes are red to symbolise Canada's sacrifice during the two World Wars. The central white stripe is bigger and represents peace. Canada's flag also contains a maple leaf, from its national tree, to show that it cares for its nature and the environment.

Adopted on July 22nd 1947, India's flag has three horizontal stripes. The top saffron coloured stripe is a symbol of courage and sacrifice. The middle white stripe represents truth, peace and purity. The lower green stripe represents life and prosperity. India's flag also contains a special wheel, the Ashok Chakra, which symbolises progress. This wheel has 24 spokes, one for each hour in the day.

Look at this page from an Atlas and answer the questions below.

1 Colour the embedded clause in paragraph A red and copy the full sentence out below.

_____

2 marks

2 Colour the embedded clause in paragraph B green and copy the full sentence out below.

_____

2 marks

3 Rewrite the following sentence so that it does not contain an embedded clause.

Sir Edmund Hillary, who was from New Zealand, flew the Union Jack when he conquered Mount Everest.

_____

2 marks

TOP CLASS - Punctuation - Year 5

Commas (within clauses)

You are a vexillographer (someone who loves to study flags to you and me). Look at the flags below and write about what their colours and symbols mean. Don't forget to use two commas to show where you have added your embedded clause in each of your sentences.

Flying the Flag:

At least one colour seen on the Olympic flag can be found in the national flag of each country of the world.

Extra information: the five interlocking rings representing the five continents of Earth.

The thirteen red and white stripes on America's flag represent the thirteen British colonies that declared independence from Britain on July 4th, 1776.

Extra information: affectionately known as 'Old Glory'.

The French flag is quite a simple flag and the three colours are often linked with the three ideals of the French Revolution: liberty, equality and fraternity.

Extra information: known as the tricolour.

The iconic flag of Japan has a red disc placed in the centre of a white background that represents the sun.

Extra information: traditionally hoisted up on a bamboo pole.

Homework

Look at the Union Jack. Why is it designed in this way? Which parts of the flag belong to which parts of the UK? Draw the four flags for the four parts of the UK and describe how they come together to form our national flag.

Commas (within clauses)

Look at the different flags of the world. Choose your favourite design and write about it. What country (or organisation) uses this flag? When was it created? By who? What do the colours represent? Are there any symbols on this flag? What do they mean?

Name:　　　　　　　　　　　　　　　　　**Date:**

My Favourite Flag

Country:

Design Date:

_____

_____

_____

_____

_____

_____

Inverted Commas

Think about...
When do we observe Remembrance Sunday?
Why do we hold this special service?
Where is your war memorial in your community?
How might this service be reported?
How and why would speech marks be used when doing so?

Guided

You are talking about Remembrance Sunday.

What do you already know about this annual event? What would you like to know? How might you find out more about this special day? Discuss this with your class teacher.

Once done, write down a set of questions that you would like to find the answers to as part of your class topic.

Then answer the questions on page 33.

Independent

You are a reporter collecting quotes to use in a newspaper article you are writing.

On your own, with a partner or in a small group; complete the task sheet provided to you by your teacher on page 34.

Once finished, cut off the homework task to take home with you for further practice.

Extension

Write a newspaper report about a local event that happened to your school. Complete the task sheet on page 35.

Once completed, publish your report on the computer.

Answers

1. The writer uses speech marks here to show us that he has taken this text from an old newspaper and not written these words himself.

2. Speech marks used here indicate that this was a common phrase used by people at the time to describe the war itself.

3. The use of speech marks here help us to identify which Latin and Greek parts of speech relate to the English word and how each word is constructed.

Homework

- No specific answers are required for this task, though teachers should check that the newspaper article chosen by each learner contains at least one example of a quote.

Remember...
We use **inverted commas** (or **speech marks**) when quoting the words that somebody has spoken (or written) in a newspaper article or a common phrase or nickname people often use when describing a specific person or event.

Inverted Commas

LEST WE FORGET

WWI (the 'war to end all wars') had been raging for four years. More than 8 million soldiers had lost their lives and countless others were badly injured. On the 11th day of the 11th month, 1918, it was agreed that the fighting would cease. An Armistice+ was signed and at 11am the guns fell silent. Each year on Remembrance Sunday (the Sunday closest to November 11th) special services are held at war memorials and churches to remember the fallen. A national ceremony takes place at the Cenotaph++ in Whitehall, London, where poppies (a symbol of remembrance) are worn and wreaths laid. A two-minute silence is also observed; it is a time for us to remember all those who have died in conflict (soldiers and civilians) and to show our gratitude for the freedom and peace they have helped to secure despite not coming home.

> 'The first stroke of eleven produced a magical effect. Someone took off his hat and...the rest of the men bowed their heads also...An elderly woman, not far away, wiped her eyes and a man beside her looked white and stern. Everyone stood very still...The hush deepened. It spread over the whole city...'
>
> **Manchester Guardian, 12th November 1919**

+ Armistice: comes from the Latin 'arma' meaning 'weapons' and 'sistere' meaning 'stop'.
++ Cenotaph: comes from the Greek 'kenos' meaning 'empty' and 'taphos' meaning 'tomb'.

Look at this article and answer the questions below.

1 Why are speech marks used in the newspaper article?

_____

_____ *2 marks*

2 Why are speech marks used in paragraph one?

_____

_____ *2 marks*

3 Why are speech marks used in the footnotes for *Armistice* and *Cenotaph*?

_____

_____ *2 marks*

TOP CLASS - Punctuation - Year 5   33

Inverted Commas

You are a reporter collecting quotes for a newspaper article you are writing about a storm. This has caused a large oak tree to come down on the roof of a school. What does each person interviewed say? Write their words in the speech bubble. Don't forget to add speech marks when you quote them.

Quotes:

Officer Welsby told reporters at a news conference

Pat Jones, Head teacher of St. Monica's, spoke of her disbelief

An angry parent, who did not wish to be named, spoke of her horror

Alex Whitehead, a Year 5 pupil, spoke of his shock

Councillor Meadows read out a statement urging everyone to remain calm

Local resident Alice Norris, who saw the tree fall, is quoted as saying

---

Homework

Look at a local or national newspaper. Find an article that includes a quote. Cut it out and highlight the quote. Underline who it was that spoke these words and think about why you think the reporter has included this quote in their article.

Inverted Commas

You are a journalist reporting on the storm. How will you tell your readers what happened at the school? Which quotes will you include in your article? Why have you chosen these quotes? How will you show your readers that these are their words and not yours?

Name: **Date:**

The Daily Post
85p

Treemendous Escape as Storm Hits School!

Reporter:

Pupils had a lucky escape yesterday when a tree crashed into their classroom during a storm that saw gusts reach up to 100mph.

Apostrophes (for omission)

Think about...
Look at this:
You're goin' out? But it's rainin'!
Is this more likely to be spoken or written?
Why do you think this? How has the writer used apostrophes to convey speech?

Guided

Imagine you are listening to a traditional Music Hall song.

Write 'I am Henry' on your wipe board. Now listen to your teacher sing the first line of the song. What do you notice? Does this make the song formal or informal? What does it tell us about the singer and the audience? Listen to the song as a whole. Copy the East End of London (Cockney) accent as you learn to sing the song itself. Get into character! What do you notice about the title?

Once you can sing the song as a real Cockney, answer the questions on page 37.

Independent

Chris has written an email to a friend.

On your own, with a partner or in a small group; complete the task sheet provided to you by your teacher on page 38.

Once finished, cut off the homework task to take home with you for further practice.

Extension

Write an email to a friend inviting them to a BBQ at your house. Complete the task sheet on page 39.

Once complete, send it and wait for their reply!

Answers

1 **Formally:** Henry
Informally: 'Enry
(Henry: note the addition of the letter 'e' here to reflect the Cockney accent)

2 h – have, her
e – every
o – would not
a – I am
i – she is

3 Fish and Chips

Homework

- No specific answers are required for this task, though teachers should check that the examples provided include an appropriate apostrophe and that the learner not only recognises why the writer has chosen to use this informal style but is also able to suggest how it could be written more formally.

Remember...
We use an **apostrophe** to show that one or more letters have been removed. This is informal and usually reflects how a word is spoken naturally rather than how it is written down formally. The use of the apostrophe helps give your writing a relaxed and friendly tone and is usually used when writing to close friends and family.

Apostrophes (for omission)

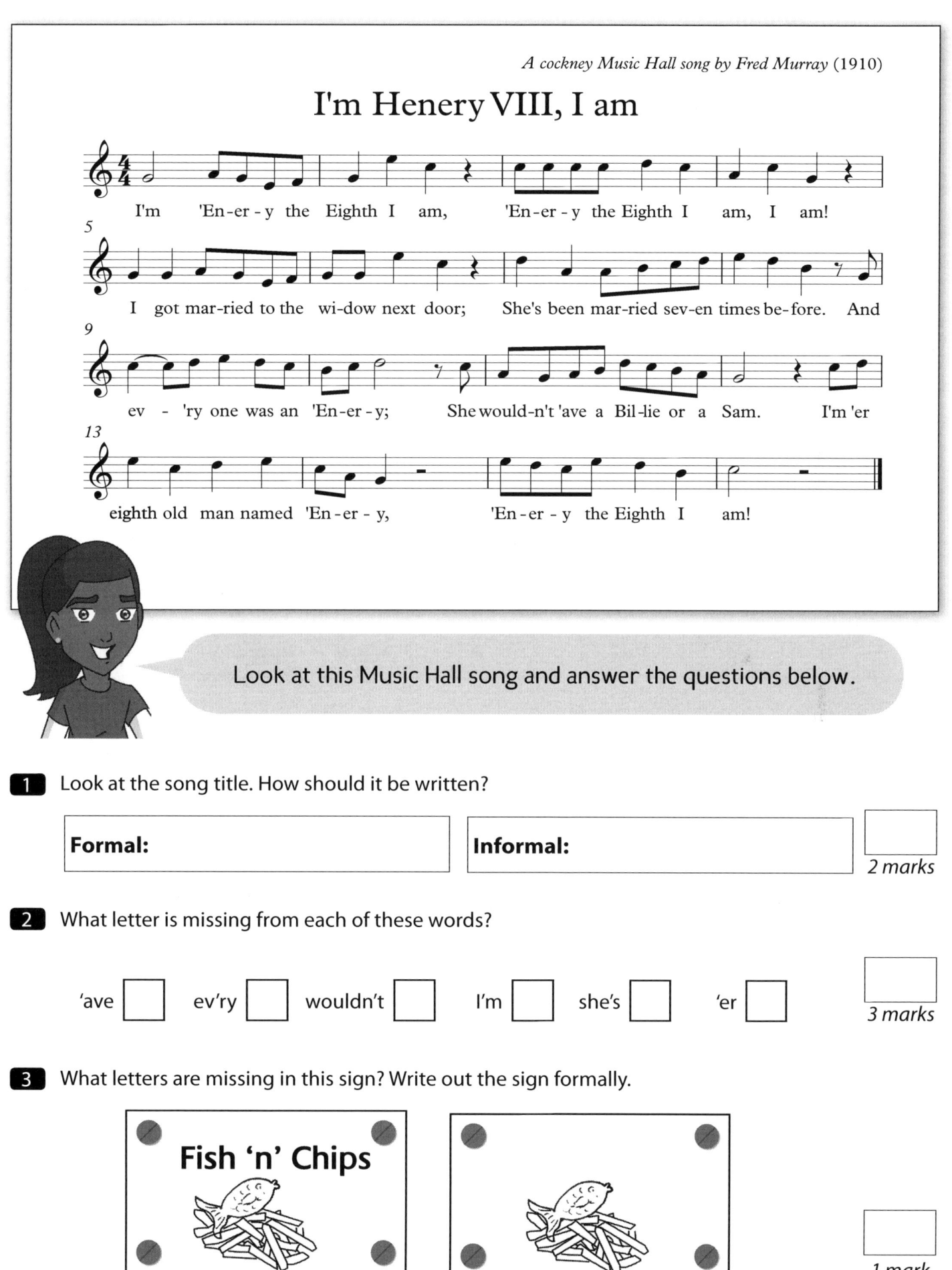

A cockney Music Hall song by Fred Murray (1910)

I'm Henery VIII, I am

I'm 'En-er-y the Eighth I am, 'En-er-y the Eighth I am, I am!
I got mar-ried to the wi-dow next door; She's been mar-ried sev-en times be-fore. And
ev-'ry one was an 'En-er-y; She would-n't 'ave a Bil-lie or a Sam. I'm 'er
eighth old man named 'En-er-y, 'En-er-y the Eighth I am!

Look at this Music Hall song and answer the questions below.

1 Look at the song title. How should it be written?

Formal:	Informal:

2 marks

2 What letter is missing from each of these words?

'ave [ ]   ev'ry [ ]   wouldn't [ ]   I'm [ ]   she's [ ]   'er [ ]

3 marks

3 What letters are missing in this sign? Write out the sign formally.

Fish 'n' Chips

1 mark

TOP CLASS - Punctuation - Year 5

Apostrophes (for omission)

You read the first draft of Chris' email to Sam and realise it's too formal. Rewrite this email.
Don't forget to use an apostrophe to contract two words together or when you are not writing the letter at all.

- Inbox (1)
- Drafts
- Sent
- Spam
- Trash

To: sam@talktalk.net
Cc:
Subject: **Blackstones Rock!!!**

Hi Sam,

Hope you are well. I have just heard tickets go on sale tomorrow for The Blackstones. I know they are your favourite band in the known universe so was wondering if you wanted to go. I am going to the Box Office with Jed first thing – we are getting the 163 if you would like to come with us.

The tickets are expensive but it will be worth it! Do not forget your Student Card as you get a £5 discount. I cannot find mine anywhere but I will keep on looking!

Meet us at the bus stop on Oxford Road (opposite Kath's Café) at half eight so we will have plenty of time to get there. Let us just hope the queues are not too long or the bus breaks down, LOL.

Give me a bell if you need to,

Chris ☺

Homework

Find an example of where an apostrophe has been used to make the following informal:
- A shop sign
- An advert
- A song lyric

Why do you think it was written in this style?
How would it be written more formally?

Apostrophes (for omission)

Write an email to a friend inviting them to come to yours for a BBQ at the weekend. What time will it start?
Will they need to bring anything?
Will there be vegetarian food available?
Who else will be there?
Will they be able to stop over?

Name:	Date:

Use the checklist below to help you write your email on the computer.

An Informal Invitation – A Checklist:

- [ ] I begin my email with 'Hi'.
- [ ] I use my friend's first name only (or their nickname).
- [ ] I place a comma after their name.
- [ ] I state why I am writing in my opening paragraph.
- [ ] I give details about the BBQ itself. This includes:
   - [ ] Where the BBQ will take place.
   - [ ] What time it will start.
   - [ ] Whether they need to bring anything (food, drink, music, toothbrush etc).
   - [ ] Telling them who else will be there.
   - [ ] Explaining what will happen if there is a downpour.
- [ ] My final paragraph encourages them to come.
- [ ] I end my email with an informal phrase.
- [ ] I sign off with my first name and use an emoticon.

TOP CLASS - Punctuation - Year 5

Apostrophes (for possession)

Think about...
What do you know about the Vikings?
When did they live?
Where did they come from?
What weapons might a Viking warrior own?
How would you show this using an apostrophe?

Guided

Imagine you discover an ancient Viking poem known as a Kenning.

What is the title of this Kenning? Who do you think Valdi is? Why? Your teacher will now show you a picture of a Viking warrior. With a partner, make a list of things that belong to Valdi the Viking. Compare your list with another group. Share your ideas with your teacher.

Once done, answer the questions on page 41.

Independent

You have made some notes on Thor, the hammer-wielding god from Norse mythology.

On your own, with a partner or in a small group; complete the task sheet provided to you by your teacher on page 42.

Once finished, cut off the homework task to take home with you for further practice.

Extension

Create a Kenning of your own. Complete the task sheet on page 43.

Once completed, learn your poem by heart and practice performing it to your classmates.

Answers

1 I. Valdi (the Viking) owns the sword

II. The use of an apostrophe ('s) indicates possession

2 Lisa's spear
James' arrow
Travis' axe

3 Chris' car had broken down.

Homework

- No specific answers are required for this task, though teachers should check that the examples provided by learners include an appropriate apostrophe to indicate a specific object is associated with a particular ancient god.

Remember...
We use an **apostrophe ('s)** to show possession. If a person's name already ends with 's' then we only need to add the apostrophe on its own.

Apostrophes (for possession)

Kennings

Originally from Norway, a kenning is an Anglo-Saxon poem; one closely associated with the Vikings.

It is like a short metaphor, each poetic phrase bringing together two words (usually with a hyphen) to describe a person or object.

Valdi's Sword

Silver – Warrior
Battle – Fighter
Blood – Spiller
Death – Bringer
Enemy – Slayer
King – Maker

Look at this page from an anthology and answer the questions below.

1 Who owns this sword? How do you know?

I. _____

II. _____

2 marks

2 How would you show who owns each of the following weapons?

Lisa owns the spear   James owns the arrow   Travis owns the axe

3 marks

3 Although both sentences are correct, which is the more formal of the two?

Chris's car had broken down.   ☐

Chris' car had broken down.   ☐

1 mark

TOP CLASS - Punctuation - Year 5   41

Apostrophes (for possession)

You have written some notes on the Viking god Thor. Use these notes to write some statements about Thor. Who was he? What did he look like? How would a Viking recognise him? Write eight statements of ownership that relate to this Viking hero.

Thor:

The 'day of Thor' 'Thor's day' = Thursday.

Many Vikings wore a hammer pendant to show they were Pagan and rejected the new religion known as Christianity.

Son of Odin (ruler of the gods).

Owned a hammer named 'Mjollnir' and wore powerful iron gloves (gauntlets).

Rode a war chariot pulled by two giant goats.

Protector of the Viking people.

Had fierce eyes and red hair.

Also chased away frosts and called upon gentle winds and warm spring rain to release the Earth from the shackles of ice and snow.

Wife = goddess Sif.

Vikings believed: thunder = rumble of his chariot, lightning = his mighty hammer in action.

A warrior god, linked to: lightning, thunder storms and strength.

Homework

Look at other gods from the ancient past:
• Ancient Egypt • Ancient Rome • Ancient Greece
Draw and label various gods, together with the object they are associated with. For example: *Anubis' scales, Mercury's winged sandals* or *Zeus' thunderbolt*.

Apostrophes (for possession)

You are a Viking poet. Write a Kenning about the character of Thor. Use your factual notes and further research to help you. How will you describe him?
What objects might he own?
What qualities does he possess?

Name: **Date:**

The Viking's Protector

Brackets

Think about...
If you could travel back in time, where would you go? Who would you visit? Why?
What would you ask them?
What might their reply be?
How might you describe this meeting at a later date?

Guided

What is the term 'sci-fi' short for? What sorts of things might you expect to see in a sci-fi adventure? Can you think of an example of this from a TV programme and film? What elements of this genre do they both have in common?

Once done, read the opening to the sci-fi book and answer the questions on page 45.

Independent

You travel back in time and find yourself on a pirate ship.

On your own, with a partner or in a small group; complete the task sheet provided to you by your teacher on page 46.

Once finished, cut off the homework task to take home with you for further practice.

Extension

You escape the pirates and travel somewhere else in time and space! Complete the task sheet on page 47.

Once completed, compare your story with that of a classmate. Share which parts of your story you like and tell each other why you like them? Select your favourite sentence to share with the class.

Answers

1 Brown = (no older than nine years old)
Yellow = (or past)

2 Allow for personal response.

3 The time traveller (despite his youthful looks) was over three hundred years old.

Homework

- 23rd November, 1963
- William Hartnell
- TARDIS
- Gallifrey

(Allow for extra information to be added to each answer but encourage that this is written within brackets to keep it separate from the main text.)

Remember...
We use **brackets** when we want to give the reader extra information in a sentence but also want to keep it separate.

44 TOP CLASS - Punctuation - Year 5

Brackets

The Keeper Arrives

Beth stood in the doorway.

A single chest sat in the very centre of an otherwise empty room.

The old man had been waiting an age for somebody to return and unlock his secrets, but when nobody did he had simply fallen asleep.

Dust had settled, cobwebs spun and spun again and the world had ambled by while he slept.

But this day was different...today he had been woken by a visitor.

He looked at the scrawny sparrow of a girl (no older than nine years old) that stood in the doorway, a key in her hand.

So his keeper had finally arrived...not what he was expecting but then life for a time traveller was full of surprises.

'I wonder if she knows what adventures we are about to go on,' he thought, relishing the thought that neither he nor the girl knew what the future (or past) had in store for them.

Beth stepped into the room and walked towards the chest.

Look at this sci-fi extract and answer the questions below.

1 Colour the brackets as follows:
Brown = gives extra information about The Keeper.

Yellow = gives extra information about where they will travel in time.

2 marks

2 Write your own sentence with a bracket in it to describe the two characters.

I. Beth: _____

II. The time traveller: _____

2 marks

3 Place brackets in the sentence below.

The time traveller despite his youthful looks was over three hundred years old.

1 mark

Brackets

You are a time traveller wandering through space and time in your time machine. Look at the sentences below and add extra information about each character you meet. Don't forget to put this information in brackets.

Shiver My Timbers!

Captain Blackbeard ruled his crew with an iron fist.		(with a temper as cruel and as ruthless as death itself)
Pirate Queen Rose was the most untrustworthy woman I had ever met.		(whose cackle would rise and fall like a thunderous curse)
Pirate Jenson's sword was a sight to behold.		(bejewelled with rubies and speckled in the blood of fallen heroes)
Caleb was rarely seen and never heard.		(the poor wretched cabin boy)
When Squawk spoke, trouble soon followed.		(Blackbeard's one true companion)

Homework

Find out about the famous time traveller Dr Who.
- When was Dr Who first broadcast?
- Who first played Dr Who?
- What is the name of Dr Who's time machine?
- What is the name of Dr Who's planet?

(Put any extra information you find in brackets)

Brackets

You escape into your time machine, just in time! Write the next chapter of your sci-fi adventure. Where will you travel? In what time period will it be set? Who will you meet? What battle will you need to fight...and win?

Name: **Date:**

THE TIME TRAVELLER

We whirled through the time corridor, a wheezing engine gasping in the depths below. As to where and when we would land, I did not know. I had barely escaped with my life but now that the controls were damaged, I could do no more than to pray that wherever we landed, it would be a place where I could repair my ship.

_____

_____

_____

_____

_____

_____

_____

Ellipses

Think about...
Look at this: Tick...tock...tick...tock...
What do you think will come next?
Why has the writer used ellipses here?
What does this suggest about how time is passing?
If you were in this story, how might you be feeling?

Guided

You are about to read a modern fable.

What features would you expect to see in a fable? What will be its purpose? How do you think such a fable will end? If this modern fable were to include animals and humans, who do you think would be the wisest? Why?

Once done, read the fable and discuss what you think the moral of the story is. Then answer the questions on page 49.

Independent

You are looking at how different writers have used ellipses effectively.

On your own, with a partner or in a small group; complete the task sheet provided to you by your teacher on page 50.

Once finished, cut off the homework task to take home with you for further practice.

Extension

Write the opening chapter of an adventure story. Complete the task sheet on page 51.

Once done, create a story to show what happens next and where your adventures lead!

Answers

1 Son followed.
The ellipses imply that the son will throw the litter on the floor too. Moreover, the repetition illustrates and emphasises that behaviour (good or bad) is learnt and that if dad wants his son to be good then he needs to set a good example.

2 b, d

3 Allow for personal response.

Homework

- No specific answers are required for this task, though teachers should check that the examples provided by each learner have included ellipses being used for each of the three reasons: to show the passage of time, to help deliver a punch line and to emphasise a repeated action.

Remember...
We use **ellipses** (...) when we want to show the passage of time for dramatic or comical effect. It can also force the reader to finish the sentence in order to make an important point or simply because the ending is an obvious one.

TOP CLASS - Punctuation - Year 5

Ellipses

MONKEY SEE, MONKEY DO

The two of them stood facing each other through the glass: man on one side, monkey on the other.

Dad leaned his head to one side and scratched his ear. Monkey did too.

Dad scrunched up his face and stuck out his tongue. Monkey did too.

Dad jumped up and down and pretended to be a chimpanzee. Monkey jumped up and down and pretended to be a man pretending to be a chimpanzee.

Dad stared deep into the eyes of the monkey to see if he understood. Monkey stared back.

"Come on, son, let's go see the elephants".

Son followed.

Dad unwrapped a sweet and popped it in his mouth.

Son followed.

Dad dropped the wrapper on the floor...

Look at this modern fable and answer the questions below.

1 What do you think the next sentence ought to be? Why?

_____

_____ *3 marks*

2 Why do you think the writer uses ellipses on the final line? Tick two boxes.
  a) He did not know how to end his story. ☐
  b) He wanted the reader to work out the end of the story themselves. ☐
  c) He wanted to give the reader a cliff hanger to make them read on. ☐
  d) He wanted to make a strong link between the title and the last
     (unwritten) line. ☐ *2 marks*

3 Do you think this was a clever way of using ellipses? Why?

_____

_____ *2 marks*

TOP CLASS - Punctuation - Year 5

Ellipses

You are looking at how different authors use ellipses effectively. Use different colours to match the two parts of text. Why do you think each writer uses ellipses rather than the words we expect to read? Once completed, put a star next to your favourite and say why you like it.

And the next line is...

A) She jumped on the back of Prince Charming's steed and, as they galloped away into the sunset, she knew what all fair maidens who have been rescued from a wicked witch or lonesome tower knew; that she would live…

B) We are not, I repeat NOT, getting a dog…

C) Sun-cream…tick. Snorkel…tick. Beach towel…tick. Flip flops…

D) It was the dead of night. Barry crept out of the window with his bag of swag over his shoulder. Nothing stirred…until, that was, those eight immortal words rang out at the foot of the ladder…

E) The tide rolls in…the tide rolls out. The tide rolls in…the tide rolls out. The tide rolls in…

F) The noise was deafening! The cows were mooing, the sheep were bleating, the horses neighing, the ducks quacking…

G) Shopkeeper: We're closed.
Shopper: I only want a pint of milk.
Shopkeeper: We're closed!
Shopper: How about for half a pint?
Shopkeeper: Do I need to say it a third time?
Shopper: OK, I get it…

H) 5…4…3…2…1…

I) A man walks into a bar…

J) With the big bad wolf dead and grandma tucked up in bed, there were only two more words left for Little Red to say…

| 1) 'ello, 'ello, 'ello. What 'ave we 'ere then? | 2) tick. | 3) WE'RE CLOSED! | 4) happily ever after. | 5) Two hours later, Fido was in the back of the car wagging his tail. |
| 6) tide rolls out. | 7) 'QUIET!' yelled Susan. | 8) Houston, we have blast off! | 9) The End. | 10) Ouch! |

Homework

Find an example of how a writer uses ellipses…
- To show the passage of time
- To help deliver a punch line
- To emphasise a repeating action

If you can't find one, write one yourself!

Ellipses

Write an adventure story. You are stopping at your grandparents over the summer holidays.
There is nothing for you to do so you decide to explore.
What do you discover?
What adventure will it take you on?

Name: **Date:**

The Rainy Day

It may have been the summer holidays but promises of glorious sunshine and thrilling adventures were nothing more than a distant memory. Boredom had come to visit in week three. It was now week five. And as the familiar sound of rain tapped on the window, it looked as though our unwelcome guest was not about to leave any time soon.

Colons

Think about...
Where might you see a clown?
What clothes might they be wearing?
What equipment might they own?
Who might you see with them?
What equipment might they have? Why?

Guided

Imagine you are about to visit the circus during the school holidays.

Which circus acts might you see? Face back to back with a partner. Give yourself two minutes to write down as many ideas as you can. After your time is up, face each other. Compare your lists. If you have an idea that your partner hasn't, you score a point. Who scores the most points?

Once discussed, make a class list with your teacher. Then answer the questions on page 53.

Independent

You are the Ringmaster and you are trying to organise the show.

On your own, with a partner or in a small group; complete the task sheet provided to you by your teacher on page 54.

Once finished, cut off the homework task to take home with you for further practice.

Extension

Design a poster advertising the circus. Complete the task sheet on page 55.

Once completed, create the poster itself.

Answers

1 It precedes a list that describes the twin girls.

2 The strongman lifted many things: a sofa, a desk and wheelbarrow full of melons.

3 Allow for personal response.

Homework

- No specific answers are required for this task, though teachers should check that the lists provided by each learner have included an appropriate colon.

Remember...
We use a **colon** to show that we are going to write a list. We can also use it after a sub-heading when it is followed by a time or set of dates to show how long an event will last.

Colons

The Strongman

The crowd fell silent. 'Mungo the Magnificent' crouched down and gripped the bar tightly. On each black orb, perched like a canary, sat one half of identical twin girls: blonde haired, buck toothed and each wearing a lemon coloured dress.

Slowly, they began to rise and when both sat high above the strongman's head, the silence gave way to rapturous applause.

'Marvel at how strong I am! No one dares challenge me, for there is nothing you can give me that I can not lift.'

He paraded his strength and his ego around the circus tent for all to see, until, that was, an old woman stepped into the ring.

The strongman stopped in his tracks and laughed.

'Do you not think I could lift you over my head with one hand, old woman?'

The crowd laughed with him.

'Oh, it is not I that I wish you to lift. It is something else which I have carried here myself. Do you accept my challenge?'

'Like taking candy from a baby,' he thought and he nodded.

Bemused, the crowd fell silent once more.

With that, the old woman reached up and took a pin from her hair and placed it at his feet.

Mungo stared at his hands; as big as dinner plates and with fingers as thick as jumbo sausages, he knew he had just been defeated.

Look at this cautionary tale and answer the questions below.

1 Why has a colon been used in paragraph one?

1 mark

2 Where should the colon go in the sentence below?

The strongman lifted many things a sofa, a desk and wheelbarrow full of melons.

1 mark

3 Write your own sentence of what the strongman lifted using a colon.

2 marks

TOP CLASS - Punctuation - Year 5

Colons

You are the Ringmaster of the Big Top. You are writing a checklist of equipment needed for each act in the show. Don't forget to use a colon before you start each list. Can you also spot where you have forgotten to include a colon in the Circus Running Times? There are four missing for you to find.

Roll up! Roll up!

CIRCUS RUNNING TIMES:

Introduction: 19:30 – 19:40

Lion Tamer: 19:40 – 20:00

Acrobats 20:00 – 20:30

Break: 20:30 – 20:50

Clowns: 20 50 – 21:15

Strongman: 21:15 – 21:40

Acrobats: 21:40 – 22 20

Clowns: 22:20 – 22:45

Finale 22:45 – 23:00

Homework

Make a list under the following sub-headings:
- Films I have seen at the cinema
- Places I have been to on holiday
- Books I have enjoyed reading
- Things I like to do in my spare time

Colons

Design a poster to advertise the circus coming to town. What dates will you be visiting? What time is each show? What acts will there be to see? How will they dazzle you? What else will there be for you to enjoy?

Name: **Date:**

ROLL UP, ROLL UP
FOR THE GREATEST SHOW ON EARTH!

Semi-colons

Think about...
Look at this sentence: For those whose day is like a stormy sea; give them calm.
What genre of text do you think it comes from?
Why do you think the writer chose to use a semi-colon and not a full stop to separate the two clauses?

Guided

Imagine you have been given a prayer to read out at a school assembly.

First, read the prayer quietly in your head. Should you read it slow or fast? Why? Which words do you think you should stress? Why? When should you pause and for how long? Why is this important? How has the writer of this prayer helped show you when this should be done? What other aspects of your reading voice will you need to consider (pitch, power, pace and volume)? Practice reading the prayer out loud to a partner.

Once done, answer the questions on page 57.

Independent

You want to write you own prayer modelled on the one you read in assembly.

On your own, with a partner or in a small group; complete the task sheet provided to you by your teacher on page 58.

Once finished, cut off the homework task to take home with you for further practice.

Extension

Write a prayer that can be read out in a school assembly. Complete the task sheet on page 59.

Once done, collect all the prayers together to make a class Prayer Book. Use these prayers in school assemblies or in class at the end of an RE lesson.

Answers

1 It helps separate the two clauses: the first focusing on the person in distress, the second focusing on what God can provide. Moreover, the semi-colon forces the reader to pause for a long time.

2 Allow for personal response. The same sentence structure and use of the semi-colon ought to be applied in order for full marks to be awarded.

3 James lit the candle; it flickered as a symbol of hope and remembrance in the wind.

Homework

- No specific answers are required for this task, though teachers should check that the sentence provided by each learner has included a semi-colon. Where possible, this sentence should also have been rewritten so that the two clauses have swapped position but the sentence as a whole still makes sense.

Remember...
It is very rare we use a **semi-colon**. It is half way between a comma and a full stop and acts as a strong pause that links two parts of a sentence.

Semi-colons

A Prayer

 God,

For those whose day is like a windswept mountain; give them comfort.

For those whose day is like a stormy sea; give them calm.

For those whose day is like the darkest night; give them hope.

For those whose day is like a battlefield; give them peace.

For those whose day is like a lonesome walk; give them joy.

Look at the prayer and answer the questions below.

1 Why has the writer used a semi-colon in each line of their prayer?

_____

_____ *2 marks*

2 Write another line for the prayer. Who will it be for? What will you ask to be given?

_____ *2 marks*

3 Where would you place the semi-colon in this sentence? Tick one box.

James lit the candle it flickered as a symbol of hope and remembrance in the wind

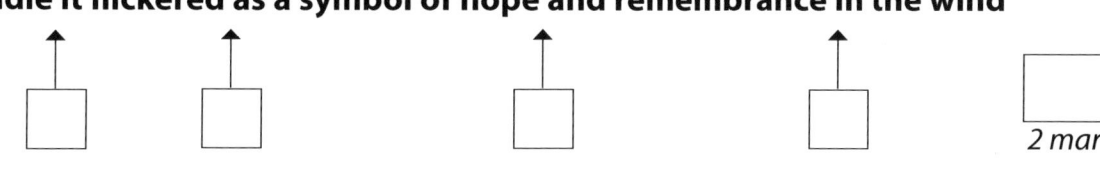

2 marks

Semi-colons

You are writing a first draft of a prayer that will be read out in assembly. You have already put down your ideas and want to match two parts to form each line of your prayer. Don't forget to use a semi-colon to show the reader when to pause between each clause.

A Prayer:

For those who are	scared	;	give them	water
	hungry			strength
	thirsty			contentment
	weak			love
	jealous			forgiveness
	unloved			food
	truly sorry			peace

1. For those who are weak; give them strength.

2. _____

3. _____

4. _____

5. _____

6. _____

Homework

Look at the book you are currently reading from your school or class library. Find three examples of a sentence that uses a semi-colon.

Semi-colons

Write a prayer of your own that can be read out in a school assembly. Who do you want to pray for? How can God help them? How will you help the reader pause between these two aspects of each line of your prayer?

Name: **Date:**

O God, hearer of prayers,

I ask unto you:

Punctuation for Parenthesis

Think about...
Why do people read books?
Write your ideas in a list. How and why might you use the following:
* Numbers   * Letters   * Full stops   * Brackets
What might happen if they weren't used?

Guided

Your teacher has asked you to make a list of the books you have read in Year 5.

How would you record this information? What heading might you give it? How would you make your list easy to read? Show your list to a partner and compare how they have written their list with your own. Which is easier to read? Why?

Once done, answer the questions on page 61.

Independent

You want to make a mini-book.

On your own, with a partner or in a small group; complete the task sheet provided to you by your teacher on page 62.

Once finished, cut off the homework task to take home with you for further practice.

Extension

Design a 3D bookmark of your own. Complete the task sheet on page 63.

Once done, make your design following the instructions you have written.

Answers

1 9. *When the Guns Fall Silent* by James Riordan

2 12. *Road to War* by Valerie Wilding

3 We read books for many reasons: (A) for pleasure, (B) to learn, (C) to help us understand and (D) to empathise with others in the hope of becoming a better person.

Homework

- No specific answers are required for this task, though teachers should ensure that opportunity is given for learners to share and discuss their mini-books. Further discussion as to the importance of following instructions in chronological order and how punctuation for parenthesis in the instructions helped us create our mini-books should also take place.

Remember...
We use a **parenthesis** to separate numbers or letters at the start of a list. When the list is inside a sentence, we use **full parenthesis** in order to enclose each number or letter.

Punctuation for Parenthesis

We read books for many reasons: (A) for pleasure, (B) to learn, (C) to help us understand and to empathise with others in the hope of becoming a better person.

Here are some books about WWI aimed at older children and teenagers:

Time to Remember

1. *Remembrance* by Theresa Breslin
2. *Eleven, Eleven* by Paul Dowswell
3. *Dusk* by Eve Edwards
4. *One Boy's War* by Lynn Huggins-Cooper
5. *Private Peaceful* and *War Horse* by Michael Morpurgo
6. *Tilly's Promise* by Linda Newbery
7. *The Edge of the Cloud* by K.M. Peyton
8. *All Quiet on the Western Front* by Erich M. Remarque
9 *When the Guns Fall Silent* by James Riordan
10. *Memoirs of an Infantry Officer* by Siegfried Sassoon
11. *The Foreshadowing* by Marcus Sedgwick

Look at this poster from a library and answer the questions below.

1 Which book is missing its punctuation for parenthesis?

_____ *1 mark*

2 How would you add *Road to War* by Valerie Wilding to the book list?

_____ *2 marks*

3 The punctuation for parenthesis (D) is missing in paragraph one. Where should it go?

_____ *2 marks*

Punctuation for Parenthesis

Put these instructions in the correct order. Don't forget to add your punctuation for parenthesis. You can choose numbers, letters or Roman numerals.

My Mini-Book:

Take a plain A4 piece of paper and fold it in half lengthways with a sharp crease.	Voilà! Your mini-book is now complete.	Take one layer of paper and fold it back on itself in order that the outer edge meets the central fold.
Carefully cut through the centre of the 'W' along the central fold, cutting through two layers of paper but stopping short at the cross field.	Turn the paper over and repeat this process so that, when finished, you end up with a 'W' shape.	You will now have an open book with four sections to it.
With your wrists above your fingers, take hold of the two halves and turn your wrists to the sides.	Unfold the paper and, again, fold it in half. Your paper should now be in four equal quarters.	Bring three of these four sections together, folding the final section on top of the other three.

Homework
Try making a mini-book. Follow the instructions carefully and write a mini-book of your own. What type of book will you write? Add illustrations. Share your mini-book with your classmates.

Punctuation for Parenthesis

You keep loosing your place in your reading book. You decide to make a 3D bookmark to solve this problem. Write an illustrated guide on how to design and make a simple bookmark. What materials will you need? What will you need to do first? What will your next step be? How will you decorate it?

Name: **Date:**

How to Make a Bookmark

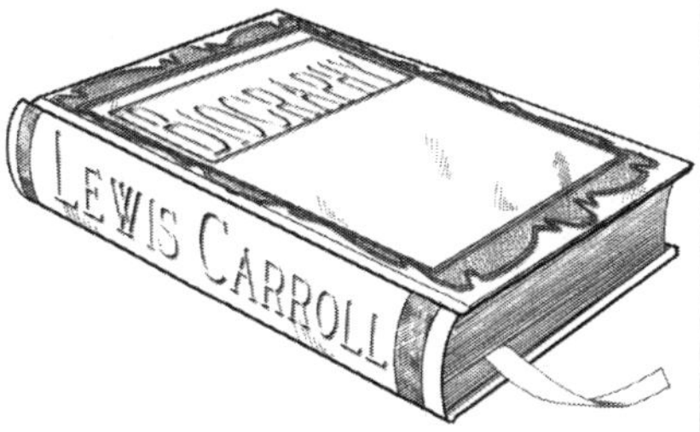

You will need:

About the author of this book

John Murray

John Murray is a recognised specialist in developing children's reading skills through interactive and kinaesthetic approaches.

Since graduating from the University of North Wales in 1997, with a Bachelor of Education degree in English and Communication, John has taught in a wide variety of schools and situations. His experience includes teaching pupils with complex language difficulties and in communities where English is not the first language. Such challenging experiences have inspired John to create innovative new approaches to the teaching and learning of Literacy; developing techniques, ideas and methods that benefit all in the classroom.

Having created the best selling *Reading Explorers* series – highly regarded in schools across Britain and sold worldwide, he balances his teaching with his work as an independent writer and lectures on how to develop key literacy skills in leading colleges and universities. He also provides both internal and external training courses for schools.

For more information regarding resources and training from John Murray visit: **www.johnmurraycpd.co.uk**